21st Century Skills **INNOVATION** *Library*

Cargo Ships

by James M. Flammang

INNOVATION IN TRANSPORTATION

Published in the United States of America by Cherry Lake Publishing
Ann Arbor, Michigan
www.cherrylakepublishing.com

Content Adviser: Amy C. Newman, Director, Forney Museum of Transportation

Design: The Design Lab

Photo Credits: Cover and page 3, ©Pieter Janssen, used under license from Shutterstock, Inc.;
page 4, ©North Wind Picture Archives/Alamy; pages 6, 15, and 25, ©Mary Evans Picture
Library/Alamy; page 9, ©sdbphoto.com/Alamy; page 10, ©Paul Thompson Images/Alamy; page
11, ©Dagmar Schneider, used under license from Shutterstock, Inc.; page 12, ©iStockphoto.com/
Norbert_Speicher; page 17, ©iStockphoto.com/Sisoje; page 18, ©David R. Frazier Photolibrary,
Inc./Alamy; page 21, ©iStockphoto.com/pastorscott; page 22, ©AP Phyoto/Heribert Proepper;
page 23, ©iStockphoto.com/SteveStone; page 26, ©iStockphoto.com/HultonArchive; page 27,
©GL Archive/Alamy; page 28, ©iStockphoto.com/Sapsiwai

Library of Congress Cataloging-in-Publication Data
Flammang, James M.
Cargo ships / by James Flammang.
    p. cm.–(Innovation in transportation)
Includes index.
ISBN-13: 978-1-60279-233-3
ISBN-10: 1-60279-233-X
1. Cargo ships–Juvenile literature. I. Title. II. Series.
HE566.F7F58 2009
387.5'44–dc22   2008008779

Cherry Lake Publishing would like to acknowledge the work of
The Partnership for 21st Century Skills.
Please visit www.21stcenturyskills.org *for more information.*

CONTENTS

INNOVATION IN TRANSPORTATION

CHAPTER ONE

Cargo Ship Beginnings

Early ships were powered by wind and human effort.

Did you ever wonder how products made in China and other faraway countries get to store shelves in your town? Or how gasoline made from crude oil produced in the Mideast ends up at your local gas station? It is likely that cargo ships played a big part in getting these products to you.

Modern cargo ships carry large amounts of goods. They transport items that are too heavy or impractical for airplanes to carry. But these shipping giants didn't develop overnight. Today's cargo ships are the result of thousands of years of innovation.

The Egyptians sent ships out to trade as early as 4000 BCE. Later, they built barges large enough to haul heavy stone objects. Egyptian barges were up to 200 feet (61 meters) long. They were the forerunners of barges used on the Mississippi River thousands of years later.

Early ships were rowed by people using oars. Soon, shipbuilders turned to wind power by installing sails. The Egyptians, for example, used square sails. But they still needed oars for times when the wind was not blowing hard enough or was blowing in the wrong direction. Soon, ships were being used by many groups for both trade and conquest.

From about 3000 to 300 BCE, a group of people called the Phoenicians engaged in sea trade. Their ships carried goods across the Mediterranean into the Atlantic Ocean.

By the eighth or ninth century BCE, the Greeks were using large galley ships for war and trade. These ships were powered by several rows of men using oars. Roman merchant ships often traveled to Egypt. They carried food and other goods for trade. By the first century BCE, they traveled to India and Africa.

The sails of a Chinese junk could be quickly opened or closed.

Over the years, **paddle wheels** were invented. These large wheels are mounted on ships and help move them through the water. The Chinese used flat-bottomed **junks**. These ships had up to five masts for sails. The junks also had watertight cargo compartments. By the ninth century CE, Chinese junks carried merchants to Indonesia and India.

From about 800 to 1070, Viking warriors and traders traveled the seas on Scandinavian longships. These ships were built with overlapping planks. This made the ships stronger. They were able to sail through heavy waves without breaking apart. The Vikings left northwest Europe and Iceland in these ships. They traveled as far as the Mediterranean Sea. Many believe that the Vikings were the first Europeans to reach North America. They would have arrived in longships.

A century or two later, caravels were cruising the Atlantic Ocean. These ships were smaller, with just two or three masts. They could sail in shallow water. Christopher Columbus's ships, the *Niña* and *Pinta*, were caravels.

The 1600s marked the beginning of the age of exploration. In 1620, the *Mayflower* brought 100 Pilgrims from Europe to New England. Most early explorers were traders as well as seekers of new lands.

Merchant ships were armed with weapons, because they often carried valuable cargo. They needed to protect themselves from pirates who roamed the seas searching for goods to steal. Several companies were formed to trade for luxury goods in the Far East.

Few realized it at the time, but the era of the sail was going to fade away. It would be replaced by ships that ran on steam power. In 1801, a steamboat called

21st Century Content

Steam powered the fleet of Liberty Ships that delivered supplies to Britain during World War II (1939–1945). Liberty Ships were developed as a reaction to German U-boat submarines. The ships were inexpensive to build and fast. On January 3, 1941, a $350 million shipbuilding program was announced, led by industrialist Henry J. Kaiser. The first Liberty Ship launched in September 1941. More than 2,700 were built in four years. Each was 441 feet (134 m) long, with five cargo holds.

the *Charlotte Dundas* ran in the Thames River in England. Robert Fulton's steamboat, the *Clermont*, made its first run in 1807 on the Hudson River in New York. Shipbuilders were eager to try steam engines on ships that could cross oceans. In 1819, the *Savannah* was the first steamship to cross the Atlantic.

Impressive as steam power was, a new way of powering engines wasn't far behind. Diesel-engine ships, running on heavy oil, appeared early in the 20th century. Before long, the era of steam also became a part of history.

CHAPTER TWO

Cargo Ship Technology

Cargo ship construction has changed a lot through the years. Shipbuilders have always looked for ways to make travel by boat easier. First, boaters realized that a longer craft was much easier to steer. **Keels** were developed, too. Positioned along the bottom of the **hull**, the keel helps keep a ship stable and upright. Oar designs changed quickly, from round sticks to flat paddles that cut sharply into the water.

Crews of workers are needed to maintain cargo ships. This ship is being repainted.

Although cargo ships made of metal are stronger than ships made of wood, they can become rusty.

Making hulls out of wooden planks, instead of a single log allowed ships to get bigger. Leakage was a problem, but innovative builders soon found a solution. They discovered that substances, such as tar, could fill the gaps and prevent water from leaking in. Shipbuilders eventually figured out how to make ships with iron hulls. This advance made cargo ships stronger and able to carry more weight.

Early sails were simple. Most were square, with limited movement. Ship operators experimented with

The rudder is a simple device. But its development greatly improved the ability of navigators to control a ship.

multiple sails and different shapes. They also learned the art of **tacking**. With this technique a ship could move forward, no matter what direction the wind was blowing.

By the 13th century, the **rudder** was used to help a ship change direction. A rudder is a flat panel attached to the stern (or rear) of a ship. When it is turned, it redirects the water. This allows the ship to turn. A person could steer using a long pole, called a tiller, that was attached to the rudder. On a modern ship, the rudder is often controlled by a cable.

Sailing ships were popular for six more centuries, until the first steam-powered ships began to cross the Atlantic Ocean. The SS *Great Britain* was designed by Isambard Kingdom Brunel. It was the first ship designed for ocean travel that had an iron hull and screw propeller. Earlier steamships used wheels. They were used most often on shorter voyages and along rivers.

Several steam-engine developments appeared around the 1860s. One was superheating. It allowed the steam generated by a boiler to be heated again. This made the engines more efficient.

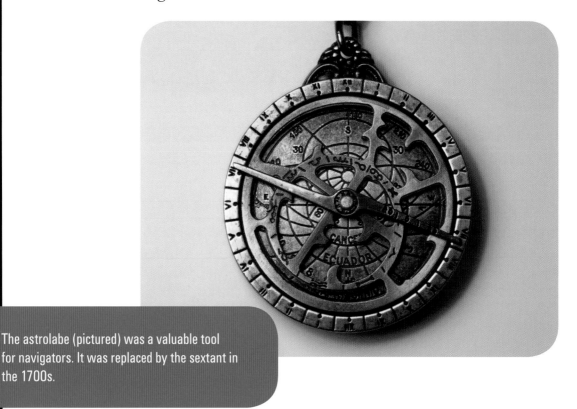

The astrolabe (pictured) was a valuable tool for navigators. It was replaced by the sextant in the 1700s.

Charles Parsons invented the steam turbine in 1884. The turbine produced more heat and was more powerful than **piston**-type steam engines. Even so, turbines would soon be replaced by diesel engines. This type of engine continues to drive most large ships today.

Navigation techniques date back to the Phoenicians, around 500 BCE. They learned to navigate by watching the positions and movements of stars in the sky. Navigators learned to plan routes and check for position along the way. For more than 2,000 years, they had little mechanical assistance except for the astrolabe. The astrolabe is a Greek invention. It helps calculate what the sun and stars will look like at a particular time and place.

By the 15th century, navigators were using the magnetic compass to help find their way. Maps and charts let navigators plan routes in advance and keep track of progress. The sextant is a mechanical device invented in the 1750s. It made it easier to determine a ship's position. Crew members on today's ships have benefited from the development of satellite technology. They use the satellites that orbit Earth as part of the Global Positioning System (GPS) to keep track of their position.

Overloaded ships were often lost at sea because they weighed too much to remain afloat. In 1876, a British

Learning & Innovation Skills

 Nuclear energy has been used to power submarines and military aircraft carriers. But only four nuclear cargo ships have ever been built. Launched in 1959, the *NS Savannah* was a project of the U.S. Atomic Energy Commission and two other agencies. Germany, Japan, and Russia also attempted nuclear cargo ships. The cost of building and operating these ships, however, has been a challenge.

In addition to the cost, some people have other concerns about nuclear-powered cargo ships. They worry about the safety of using nuclear power sources, such as uranium, in these ships. Do you think that working to develop more nuclear-powered ships is a good idea? Why or why not?

politician named Sir Samuel Plimsoll helped solve this problem. He introduced the load line. The load line showed the maximum depth to which a ship could be loaded safely.

Communicating with other ships has always been important to help avoid collisions and warn one another of danger. Sailors have used hand signals, flags, and lights to signal other vessels. The invention of wireless telegraphy at the dawn of the 20th century made it possible to contact ships that were far away. Radio, which appeared in the 1920s, made communication even easier. World War II brought radar and sonar. These technologies helped determine what was ahead of a ship or below it.

CHAPTER THREE

Business and Marketing

Early trading ships carried anything that could be sold or bartered. A load might include grains, spices, and oils. Roman ships carried oil in big ceramic jars. Spices from the Far East have been a prized item for many centuries.

Not all of the "goods" carried within ships were pleasant to think about. For centuries, enslaved people were transported by ship. In the 1700s and 1800s, the slave trade provided big profits for ship

Enslaved people endured horrible conditions when they were transported. Considered cargo, they were packed tightly into the holds of ships.

owners. Those who bought and sold the enslaved people and also made money.

Until well into the 19th century, most trading voyages were on tramp ships. Rather than start off with a full load, tramp ships traveled from port to port, seeking cargo.

Common carrier service began in 1818. To make their services more convenient, ships would sail at specific times and charge fixed rates.

In 1886, the first ship built exclusively to carry petroleum was launched. The *Gluckauf* was a coal-burning steamship with an iron hull and 16 tanks for the precious liquid oil.

Not all of the innovations in shipping had to do with building better ships. The Panama Canal opened in 1914. It made it much easier to send goods from one side of the United States to the other. Before the canal was dug, ships had to travel all the way around the southern tip of South America.

Until the early 1960s, all ships were loaded and unloaded at docks, by laborers known as **longshoremen**. Workers lifted cargo off of trucks, and put the sacks and crates onto special platforms or in nets. These were then loaded onto ships with the help of cranes. This was hard work, and it took a long time to handle each ship. Goods often were damaged, and valuable merchandise was sometimes stolen.

Traveling through the Panama Canal can shorten a ship's journey by thousands of miles.

All that began to change in 1956. That's when Malcolm McLean invented the metal shipping **container**. Container shipping allowed ships to be loaded and unloaded in a completely different way. The container is a large metal box made in standard sizes. It can be loaded at a factory or farm, sealed shut, and taken

Automobiles are unloaded from a cargo ship docked at the Port of Long Beach in California.

by truck or train to the port. At the dock, a giant crane lifts the sealed container onto the ship and places it into the cargo hold. Containers can be stacked six to eight high, inside the hold and on deck. Each one is locked into a cell, where it remains secure during the voyage. When the ship reaches its destination, other cranes lift the containers off the ship and place them on the dock.

Today, all containers are 8 feet (2.4 m) wide and 8.5 feet (2.6 m) high. They can be 10, 20, or 40 feet (3, 6, or 12 m) long. They are made of steel or aluminum, with two loading doors at one end. Computers control how and where the containers are loaded. This allows shipping companies to make the best use of the storage space on each ship. It also helps companies track each shipment.

Containerships dominate the shipping business, but other ships still are needed. Breakbulk ships handle cargo that does not fit properly into containers, such as steel and machinery. On bulk ships, grains such as wheat and rice are poured into the hold. Bulk ships also carry substances such as iron ore and coal.

Refrigerated ships, called **reefers**, hold perishable goods. They carry goods that will spoil if they aren't kept cold while they are transported. They appeared early in the 20th century and first used ice-filled compartments.

Car carriers have a boxy superstructure. This superstructure extends the full length and width of the hull. Known as ROROs (roll-on/roll-off), they are designed so vehicles can be driven aboard on a ramp. The vehicles are stored inside the ship for the ocean crossing.

21st Century Content

Many Asian car manufacturers regularly ship vehicles across oceans. Large car and truck carriers are more than 700 feet (213 m) long. Each one can carry as many as 8,000 passenger cars. Larger vessels have movable decks, so they can hold trucks. To hold as many as possible, only a 6-inch (15 centimeter) space is left between vehicles. It takes 12 to 15 days to cross the Pacific Ocean from Japan to Tacoma, Washington.

CHAPTER FOUR

The Future of Cargo Ships

The ships of today are very specialized and function well. But the future is sure to bring changes to their time-tested designs. One improvement that innovators are working on is greater fuel efficiency. Because ships are extremely heavy, they consume huge amounts of expensive fuel.

Over the past several decades, ships have been getting bigger. This allows them to carry more cargo. They require more fuel than their smaller cousins. As the 21st century began, the largest ship on Earth was the tanker *Jahre Viking*. It is 1,503 feet (458 m) long and capable of holding 541,000 tons (490,787 t) of oil. The 1,303-foot (397 m) *Emma Maersk*, was launched in 2006. It is the biggest containership in the world. The huge ship requires a crew of just 13 people.

A tanker is a specially designed cargo ship that can hold large amounts of liquid. Some tankers are designed to transport dry cargo.

Supersize ships can now haul approximately 6,000 steel containers. A new class of ultra-large ships could appear soon, capable of holding 9,000 containers. Even bigger ships are being considered.

Someday, solar power might run large ships. Nuclear power could be tried again. Or a completely new power source might be developed. Until then, shippers search for innovative ways to reduce fuel consumption.

SkySails offers its kite system for cargo ships and other large ships, such as yachts.

A few are reverting to wind power. SkySails, a German company, developed a parasail wind-**propulsion** system. The parasails look like giant kites. When they are raised to about 1,500 feet (457 m), they provide considerable pulling force to help the diesel engine. Fuel costs can be cut by 10 percent to 35 percent, according to SkySails. In January 2008, the kite-assisted

MS *Beluga* made its first voyage. The ship sailed from Germany to Venezuela. During use of its kites, SkySails estimated the ship saved 20 percent on fuel consumption when it used its kites.

Further into the future, cargo ships might even be capable of going under water, like submarines. In addition, ships that ride on a cushion of air, rather than sit deeply in the water, could come into greater use.

For now, pollution is another issue that needs attention. Like cars and trucks, ships also emit pollutants that can contribute to global warming. People concerned about the environment claim that oceangoing vessels account for 2 percent to 3 percent of global fuel consumption. They produce 14 percent of the world's nitrogen emissions from fossil fuels and 16 percent of the sulfur emissions from petroleum. Cargo ships run on a low-cost fuel that environmentalists say is the worst pollutant. One containership, they insist, pollutes the air more than 2,000 diesel-engine trucks.

Learning & Innovation Skills

As ships become more efficient and carry more cargo, one thing is lost: beauty. Few of today's ships can compare to the sight of an old schooner or clipper ship with its sails full of wind. The ships of tomorrow might not be beautiful to look at, but they will probably do their jobs more efficiently.

Do you think ship designers should worry more about how a ship looks or how much cargo it can carry? Do you think it is possible to design ships that are both functional and beautiful?

Oil spills are a concern, too. An oil tanker that has an accident and leaks can spew millions of gallons of harmful liquid into the ocean. In 1989, the *Exxon Valdez* sent millions of gallons of crude oil into Prince William Sound, off the coast of Alaska. Since 1990, U.S. tankers carrying crude oil have needed an inner and outer hull. This provides better protection against leaks. Innovators continue to work on ways to make oil spills less likely.

An oil spill from a tanker can affect the environment for years.

CHAPTER FIVE

Some Important Innovators

Using a sextant is sometimes referred to as "shooting the sun."

Many people through the years have contributed to the development of cargo ships as we know them. Here are just a few of them.

John W. Hadley

Without navigation skills, ship captains could never have found their way to new destinations. John W. Hadley was an English mathematician. He was one of two men who invented the sextant. By calculating positions of the sun, moon, and stars, the sextant could determine the ship's latitude. That's the distance from the equator.

James Watt

Scottish engineer James Watt deserves praise for his invention of the steam engine. It eventually helped speed up ocean travel. His developments played a key role in the Industrial Revolution. The watt, a measurement of energy, is named for him.

Watt, pictured here as a child, enjoyed reading and making mechanical toys in his father's carpenter shop.

Brunel didn't just design ships. He is also famous for designing a network of tunnels and bridges for British trains.

Isambard Kingdom Brunel

Isambard Kingdom Brunel was a British engineer. He designed three notable ships, along with 100 bridges and 25 railway lines. One of his creations, the SS *Great Britain*, was the first iron-hulled oceangoing ship with a propeller.

Malcolm McLean

Born to a farming family in North Carolina, Malcolm McLean had a trucking business. While waiting at the docks in Hoboken, New Jersey, in 1937, he watched the ships being loaded. Many workers were needed to handle the separate crates. It took a long time to load the ship. He wondered if there could be a better way. After selling

The introduction of standard containers made shipping cargo more practical and efficient.

his trucking firm in 1955, McLean bought a shipping company. He renamed it Sea-Land. He purchased two oil tanker ships and modified them to hold large container boxes.

In April 1956, a ship called *Ideal-X* left Newark, New Jersey. It had 58 preloaded containers on board, and was bound for Houston, Texas. In 1966, McLean's company made its first shipment across an ocean. His invention changed the entire course of shipping, making it much more efficient and profitable.

Life & Career Skills

Malcolm McLean's containers prove that innovations don't have to be complicated. Getting the idea isn't enough, though. The innovator has to make it work. McLean had to find ways to adapt ships to hold containers. This included strengthening their decks. Massive cranes were needed to lift the containers, which could be stacked both down in the cargo hold and on the deck. McLean and others came up with standard sizes for containers. That way they would stack neatly into the ship and remain secure during the voyage. Without problem-solving skills and the ability to work with others to reach a goal, even an innovator's best new idea can fail.

Glossary

container (kuhn-TAYN-er) in shipping, a large metal box that can be filled with goods and loaded onto a ship along with many other similar-size boxes

holds (HOHLDZ) large compartments below the deck where cargo is stored

hull (HUHL) the frame or body of a ship

junks (JUNGKS) flat-bottomed Chinese sailing ships

keels (KEELZ) projections that run along the bottom of boats and help keep them balanced

longshoremen (LAWNG-shor-men) workers who load and unload ships at a dock

navigation (na-vuh-GAY-shun) the act of determining the course of a vehicle

paddle wheels (PAD-uhl-weelz) wheels with boards or paddles around the rim, used to propel a ship; they can be located at the side or rear of a ship

piston (PISS-tuhn) a cylinder that moves back and forth inside a larger cylinder

propulsion (pruh-PUHL-shuhn) the act of propelling, or moving something forward

reefers (REEF-urz) ships with refrigerated cargo compartments for carrying perishable goods

rudder (RUHD-ur) flat vertical panel used to steer a ship

schooner (SKOO-nur) a fast, narrow-hulled ship with two masts and sails that run lengthwise

tacking (TAK-ing) changing the direction of a ship by moving its sails

For More Information

BOOKS

Graham, Ian. *Ships*. New York: Franklin Watts, 2007.

Rebman, Renée C. *Robert Fulton's Steamboat*. Minneapolis: Compass Point Books, 2008.

Sutherland, Jonathan, and Diane Canwell. *Container Ships and Oil Tankers*. Pleasantville, NY: Gareth Stevens Publishing, 2008.

WEB SITES

Boomerang Box—Trade Topics: The History of Cargo Ships
www.apl.com/boomerangbox/d1117.htm
Learn more about the history of cargo ships

Extreme Engineering—Container Ships: Harbor Pilot
video.aol.com/video-detail/extreme-engineering-container-ships-harbor-pilot/400553854
Watch a video of a harbor pilot guiding a containership safely into harbor

Index

About the Author

James M. Flammang is a journalist and author who specializes in transportation topics. Technology is one of his primary interests. He enjoys writing about technical achievements of the past, as well as those that may come in the future. In addition to evaluating and reviewing new cars and trucks, he has written more than 20 books about the history of the automobile. His Web site, Tirekicking Today, has been at www.tirekick.com since 1995. In addition to titles in the Innovation in Transportation series, he has written three previous books for young readers. Flammang lives in Elk Grove Village, Illinois.